IDEAS IN PSYCHOANALYSIS

Sublimation

Kalu Singh

Series editor: Ivan Ward

ICON BOOKS UK

TOTEM BOOKS USA

Published in the UK in 2001
by Icon Books Ltd., Grange Road,
Duxford, Cambridge CB2 4QF
E-mail: info@iconbooks.co.uk
www.iconbooks.co.uk

Published in the USA in 2001
by Totem Books
Inquiries to: Icon Books Ltd.,
Grange Road, Duxford
Cambridge CB2 4QF, UK

Sold in the UK, Europe, South Africa
and Asia by Faber and Faber Ltd.,
3 Queen Square, London WC1N 3AU
or their agents

Distributed to the trade in the U
by National Book Network Inc.,
4720 Boston Way, Lanham,
Maryland 20706

Distributed in the UK, Europe,
South Africa and Asia by
Macmillan Distribution Ltd.,
Houndmills, Basingstoke RG21 6XS

Distributed in Canada by
Penguin Books Canada,
10 Alcorn Avenue, Suite 300,
Toronto, Ontario M4V 3B2

Published in Australia in 2001
by Allen & Unwin Pty. Ltd.,
PO Box 8500, 83 Alexander Street,
Crows Nest, NSW 2065

ISBN 1 84046 272 8

Text copyright © 2001 Kalu Singh

The author has asserted his moral rights.

Series editor: Ivan Ward

Typesetting by Hands Fotoset

Printed and bound in the UK by
Cox & Wyman Ltd., Reading

Introduction: Better Mind the Bollocks

If the head's sublime, then what the fuck? Here is a working-class poet-painter's answer:

The head Sublime, the heart Pathos, the genitals Beauty, the hands & feet Proportion.[1]

It is a riddle to tease the Sphinx. But is it a riddle or a reminder? For when one first reads Blake's 'Proverb (of Hell)' in adolescence, everything fits – except the third phrase. Yes, the high, mind-holding head must be Sublime; and the bleeding heart, Pathos; and Leonardo's 'Vitruvian Man' of outstretched limbs, that ancient puzzle of squaring the circle, is all about Proportion. But how to see Beauty in the genitals? Wouldn't the more obvious noun be 'danger', or – in the anti-sexual Christian dispensation – 'sin', or even 'Eve's sin', or 'corruption'? Or, in the mundane efflorescence of puberty, simply 'urgency'? Yes, the narcissist thinks of Beauty – but what of the Other's genitals? So does the pervert – but what of the Self's? Isn't the strongest sensation that of puzzlement which, as it gropes towards clarity, becomes anxiety? Looking at or thinking about the genital flesh-lock, something does seem to fit, literally, and yet there is a residue of sensation and thought. Sigmund Freud called this 'the uncanny', and stated more boldly that 'the genitals are hardly ever judged to be beautiful'.[2] But when we can see how Beauty comes in, are we also saying that the Sublime must be excluded from the genitals? And what are 'Beauty' and the 'Sublime' anyway – and aren't all these terms from art and not anatomy?

Somehow, at some point, one learns how to use the sentence, 'This is beautiful.' It is rare to remember this as a specific experience. It is lost among the experiences of learning how to say 'This is tasty/nice/lovely.' Virginia Woolf's 'hero-ine' Orlando is startled to find that his Turkish gypsy hosts have no such word as 'beautiful'. Their equivalent phrase translates as 'How good to eat!'[3] Nor did the English have such a word until Tyndale minted it for his new Bible.[4] But he didn't mint the obvious pairing for it – 'uglyful'. Orsino's lament, 'If music be the food of love',[5] expresses how different modalities of appetite – aesthetic, sexual and plain hunger – can both substitute for each other and also fuse: but why do they?

It seems that all human societies develop such terms as 'beauty' and 'sublime' to mark out some specific experiences. The other puzzle about these terms is that they carry an ethical evaluation: to say that some

4

thing or some relationship is beautiful or ugly carries a moral charge. There are three approaches to their use:

1. Aesthetics – this states the conditions of ascription of such terms to:
   a) the objects out there, whether of Nature or made by men and women.
   b) the inner experience, individual or shared, occasioned by the making or attention to these objects. It delineates the intellectual faculties and the range of emotions involved.
2. Developmental Psychology and Sociology – this describes how individuals learn to make such ascriptions, and the cultural values they embody. It is explanation at the inter-personal level.
3. Psychoanalytic Theory – this proposes an explanation at the intra-personal level: what is happening inside the individual to facilitate such experiences. Its core concept is *sublimation*. I will argue that this psychoanalytic concept offers a genuine contribution to the understanding of what is going on in these experiences and the use of these terms which was opened up by ethics and aesthetics.

Let us return to ordinary usage and see how desire,

aggression and anxiety are inscribed in these terms. The limiting experience of anxiety is the sense of annihilation of the integrity of the Self. One might say that there are two poles here: before birth, the anxiety is pure physical emotion; before death, it is pure intellection – 'When I have fears that I may cease to be.'[6] These would seem two obvious candidates for the sublime, but in fact ordinary life treats them as enigmas to avoid wasting energy upon. The more insistent diurnal anxiety is about frustration of desire and managing the consequential aggression. Thinking again of Blake's mirror, anatomically the head and the genitals are well separated: perhaps the heart is at the mediating midpoint. But (male) slang shows an anxiety about the impossibility of separation: 'penis-brain' and 'dickhead' are terms of abuse only marginally less scornful than 'wanker'. There are no female equivalents such as 'vagina-brain' or 'twat-head'; and nor does 'prick' resonate with as much aggression as 'cunt', whether spoken by straight or gay men. For some men, the ultimate terror is to be *marked* as a woman. Even Queen Noel Coward appropriated heterosexual anxiety when he called Kenneth Tynan 'a cunt'.[7]

Women, in their turn, appropriate male definitions. Voltaire doubted a woman's ability to imagine the highest themes, because he believed that 'The composition of a tragedy requires testicles'.[8] Two centuries on, actress Helen Mirren, asked why she liked her female lead in David Hare's new play about a rock-chick, *Teeth 'N' Smiles*, replied: 'It's got balls!' 'And', teased the interviewer, 'that's good for a woman?'[9] A colleague, who aspired to be a writer, reported an adult dream of castration, which included the additional distress that he couldn't write with his newly cut member – pen-as-envy or writer's cock-block!

Again, some kind of experience of exchange or fusion between the physical and the intellect is being adumbrated here, as is the age-old anxiety of insufficiency of balls or even castration. The reader might already be annoyed at this familiar psycho-analytic melding. Here is a clever and scrumptious refutation of such scepticism. Knowing that the Germans had executed 15,000 of their own soldiers during the Second World War for an indiscipline which the Allies were recognising as post-traumatic stress disorder, Anthony Storr was interested to meet, in 1948, one of their psychiatrists who was visiting the Maudsley Hospital. He remembers the latter 'boasting that war neurosis was virtually non-existent in the German forces, and affirming that

Freud's theories were nonsense. We asked him how they managed cases of incipient breakdown. "We threatened them with castration: that soon got them back in line", he replied.'[10]

How perfectly this echoes the British Tommy's fantasy about the defeatable enemy.

Hitler has only got one ball:
The other is in the Albert Hall.
His mother, the dirty bugger,
She chopped it off when he was small.[11]

If envy, greed and fear of the Other's possessions are the ordinary shadows of broken desire, what is ordinary health but sharing and gratitude or, in Joan Riviere's phrase, 'welcome by gratification'?[12] It took Hollywood almost the entire first century of cinema to attain the courage to show this: in *Boogie Nights,* a young woman says to her lover, 'Your cock is so beautiful'.[13] I've yet to see a parallel celebration of the vagina. The nearest was in the TV sitcom *Third Rock From The Sun*, in which the alien Sally misunderstands a reference to Mesopotamia as to her own 'fertile crescent'.[14]

Let us begin by seeing how far aesthetics takes us.

Kunstry Matters: the Philosophical Sublime

Pretty-boy David defeated the Gentile giant, but the war between aesthetes and philistines is perennial – creating anxiety, resentment and anger on both sides. The philistines, with the wrath of the excluded and indolent, swear: 'We don't care if you ponces don't call it Art – we like it!' Like Humpty Dumpty, they assume the right to name and define at will. The space they find for the sublime seems to treat it as a synonym for '*very* beautiful'. From their elegant temples, the aesthetes insist on rites of passage requiring considerable learning and humility. Aesthetics begins by separating the 'useful/functional' from the 'beautiful', and the latter from the 'sublime'.

Hamlet's teasing pun to Ophelia, 'Do you think I meant country matters?',[15] is the nearest Shakespeare came to the most fearful word in the vernacular. The euphonious virgin-philosopher Kant was famously more interested in *Kunst* (Art). His masterly aesthetics argues that the faculties of Imagination, Understanding and Reason which process (sense) data from the external physical world and the internal mental world can – and in fact must – be used not only to gain conceptual knowledge and to inform practical action but also in what he calls 'harmonious free play'.[16] The aesthetic delight in, say, a tulip is disinterested and purposeless, and so is distinguishable from any interested pursuit of agreeable sensations of the tulip as Good – worthy or perfect. 'Delight in the beautiful must depend upon the reflection on an object precursory to some (not definitely determined) concept.'[17] This notion of being able to live with and enjoy a pre-conceptual or conceptually uncertain state anticipates Keats's brilliant idea of 'negative capability' ('when man is capable of being in uncertainties, Mysteries, doubts, without any irritable reaching after fact & reason'[18]) as an aspirational moral as well as aesthetic developmental marker. It also looks forward to Bion's recommendation that the therapist enter the therapeutic space 'without memory and desire . . . and with a capacity for reverie'.[19]

For Kant, the perception of form and limitation which characterises experiences of the beautiful, whether of the tulip or the abstract painting, induces in the mind a sense of being 'in *restful* contemplation'.[20] On the other hand, the Sublime experience is of the mind 'set in motion', beginning as 'a rapidly alternating repulsion and attraction produced by one and the same Object' of seemingly limitless (mathematical) magnitude or seemingly formless (dynamic) might – for example, the starry cosmos or the volcanic storm or high tragedy; and moving from humiliating terror to an invigorating awareness of the power of Reason, the faculty of ideas which can explain, contain and help to transcend that initial emotional disarray.[21] Kant introduces the concept of 'subreption' for this 'substitution of a respect for the Object in place of one for the idea of humanity in our own self – the Subject'.[22] The theme of substitution is germane to our project.

Though he further highlights the difference from the beautiful by calling the sublime 'a negative pleasure', it is through the latter concept, and its grounding in ideas, that Kant delineates the worth of human-made art. 'We say of a man who remains unaffected in the presence of what we consider sublime that he has no (moral) feeling.'[23] The task of the artist – and here Kant means 'original artist' and not merely 'imitator' or 'hack' – is to generate aesthetic ideas. These products of the free play of her imagination and understanding are what he calls 'inexponible': though there is an intuitive sense of a fit between the ideas and the work made, the concepts of understanding cannot explain it.[24] From the spectator's side, the inadequacy of concepts in relation to aesthetic pleasure is familiar: one runs out of worthwhile things to say about the final meaning of Virgil or Mozart.

For Kant, the presence 'proximately or remotely' of moral ideas, rather than 'sensation (charm or emotion)', is what makes a man-made object aesthetically worthwhile. His absolute belief in this can be seen in his aphorism: 'The beautiful is the symbol of the morally good.'[25] In the following two remarks he is making a developmental as well as moral point. 'Hunger is the best sauce . . . [but] . . . Only when men have got all they want can we tell who among the crowd has taste or not. . . . The beauties of nature are in general the most beneficial, if one is early habituated to observe, estimate and admire them.'[26]

Disinterested attention presupposes the satisfaction of desire; and desire presupposes the satisfaction of need. Some people never make the transition. It is a real question and not merely an urban aesthete's jibe to ask: 'How much of one's humanity is perverted or lost if one doesn't frequently commune aesthetically with nature?' It's common enough to feel tired of every piece of art – CD, video, painting, book – one has; and also to meet precious, vicious aesthetes. Or to ask it another way, what did Blake get when he imagined the meaning of the creation of the tiger; or today, what has my friend's eight-year-old daughter, Marika, got from her introduction to the beauty of the cockroach? It is worth remembering that one's first early habituations are so intensely to people (and nature) that one must slowly learn that not everything is as alive as oneself. Most philosophers and mystics have consistently argued for the worth of experiences of beauty, and particularly the sublime. Such a motion of the imagination is felt to be intrinsically good. But there is a sceptical strand from Plato. He famously banished poets from his ideal Republic, believing that any genuine proto-socialist realism, by depicting human weakness and depravity, would fail to be educative and inspiring.[27] We laugh nervously at anyone who banishes artists or burns books. But more astutely, and perhaps humanely, he did question our ability to contain our imagination. In speaking of *theios phobos*, sacred fear, he reminds us that this faculty of the imagination is so protean and powerful that we would do well to limit our engagement of its forces.[28] More art per day doesn't always mean more good. Music only sometimes soothes the troubled breast, and, as clinicians have pointed out, some schizophrenics have been further deranged by attempts to heal them with art.[29]

The etymology of 'sublime' includes the ideas of boundary/limit/threshold; the traverse beams in a doorframe, a lintel; a process of approach to, crossing over or emerging from the boundary; reservoir, conduit and valve. We will see below that these ideas of container and change across a boundary connect with sublimation. The physiology of the sublime, or certainly of one of the defining examples – the Cortez-like view from the mountain – tells us that during this experience we don't actually focus our eyes on the scene, and we thereby facilitate the production of alpha waves which are typically related to relaxation. It could be said that this doesn't so much reduce the sublime to the merely gratifying, but frees the energy for the associative thinking which leads to a conceptual recognition of the sublime.[30] Chiming with these descriptions are the basic prescriptions to therapists of mental unfocusing – free-floating, evenly suspended attention, the third ear, etc. So we come to psychoanalysis.

Sexual Annealing: Freud's Account of Sublimation

Freud's theoretical paper on 'Sublimation' was lost – disappeared into thin air! All that remain are scattered remarks in various other papers. The best way into any psychoanalytic concept is through the Oedipus complex. Between the cosy fantasy of a man and woman simply having sex and then nurturing the resultant baby until it is old enough to have sex and make its own babies, and the lived experience – marked in countless narratives – of profound puzzlement and distress in the nuclear nest, Freud and Melanie Klein saw a cauldron of terrifying desires, thoughts and emotions that ordinary conceptions didn't dare approach. It feels strange arguing for the heuristic worth of the complex. But if I must, I ask the reader to try to understand, let alone explain, the following vignettes *without* recourse to psychoanalytic concepts. What kind of person, what kind of artist, is being described? What did their creative impulse mean?

a) Hank is the chat-show sidekick to Larry in the TV parody-sitcom *The Larry Sanders Show*. He is obsequious and inept, a dull foil of a fool, but still desperate to be as media-cool as Larry's producer Arthur. Eventually he thinks he has something impressive: a very young beautiful woman agrees to marry him – on TV. Her father shows up for the first time at the reception. When Larry and

Arthur look up to greet him they see the spitting image of Hank. They are speechless with embarassment.[31]

b) Stephen Sondheim's parents were in the fashion trade. His father left when he was 10. His mother 'Foxy' became 'creepy . . . She would sit across from me with her legs aspread . . . would lower her blouse'. His father wanted him to 'get a proper job and not become a feckless artist'. On what she thought was her death-bed, Foxy wrote to her middle-aged son: 'The only regret I have in life is giving you birth.'[32]

c) European trash-TV viewers and Guinness Book of Records anoraks would have been introduced to Lolo Ferrari as 'the woman with the largest breasts in the world'. She also had huge bee-stung lips. In her TV cameos with Antoine de Caunes, the vicarious stud, and Jean-Paul Gaultier, the gay designer, and also in her live stage/bar shows where she invited men to touch the peaks of fantasy, she seemed to be enjoying the limitless power to fascinate and seduce accorded to those who inhabit superlatives. Even allowing for the shallow mask of celebrity, it felt reasonable to assume she got *some* sexual pleasure from these sexualised displays. But in her TV obituary, her photographer said: 'You can touch her, every part, but as soon as you touch her lips she becomes completely mad.' She confessed: 'During sex, I can't stand it when someone touches my breasts.' For her ageing mother, Lolo's androgynous husband/manager was the villain: 'The best revenge on Eric would be to pour acid on his face ... I'm going to do it.' Her father didn't speak to the camera.[33]

d) Some men, especially those who generate a public image of pork-sword wizardry, such as John Lennon, ask to call their wife 'Mother'. Why?[34]

e) At the age of 25, Salvador Dalí exhibited two paintings: 'Sometimes I Spit For Pleasure On The Portrait Of My Mother', and 'The Great Masturbator'. Because of the former, his father banished him from the family home.[35]

So, here we have some 'artists':

a) Sondheim – transforming word and sound into the beauty of song and theatre.

b) Lolo – transforming *herself* into a thing of sexualised beauty.

c) Hank's wife – who *found* a lost, inaccessible object of beauty and desire in a simulacrum.

d) Lennon – *projecting* an old role onto the new Other.

e) Dalí – an unbridled imagination broken by envy, ingratitude and rage, getting himself removed from what his friend Lorca called 'the jungle of blood', heterosexual intercourse.

Psychoanalysis didn't merely add adverbs and intensifiers to common concepts and narratives: 'he *really* loved his mother'. It tried to provide a correlate for the sense of mighty, almost uncontainable and unthinkable, emotions and thoughts which attend ordinary development. Perhaps, given the way aesthetic narratives work – and here again is the crucial Kantian concept of inexponible ideas – the theorists chose received narratives to present the theory. The stories of Oedipus, Elektra, Hamlet and Faust induce a sense of inexhaustible wonder which seems to fit the puzzling taste for the dark side of family life.

Hank's wife is doomed to find that the physical simulacrum of her father can only be an unsatisfying shadow of the figure in ancient fantasy. And poor Hank is doomed to learn that he can have no real existence with her. The marriage does indeed collapse within a year.

It was Sondheim's poor revenge to be famously scruffy. It was a different revenge to be a successful artist. And perhaps another different revenge to be gay. Just think of him knowing for decades, perhaps only unconsciously until the letter, that his mother wished him dead – and yet still being able to write love songs like 'Maria' and 'Tonight'.

Lolo, child slang meaning 'big tits', had a real name, Eve – the proto-mother. Eric remembered Eve saying that 'Her mother refused to breast-feed her. Lolo thought her mother wouldn't breast-feed her because her mouth wasn't pretty enough or big enough.' Her mother admitted: 'When she was born, I had an impression that I'd been reborn. She had my face, madonna features . . . but I always hated my face. . . . And I think she could feel this . . . inherited my sense of self-loathing.'[36]

As Ferrari is now dead, we can't ask when she first sensed her mother's absence of desire to offer a loving breast, and how consciously informed were her decisions to undergo plastic surgery. Twenty-two operations in five years – more than on Freud's mouth! At a trite, naïve realist level, she could now suck her own breasts, displacing her mother's. But more symbolically, she displaced them absolutely, and all women/mothers, by having the largest – and in the fantasy equation, most-wanted – breasts in the world.

What seemed missing from her understanding was her rage at, and despair of, her father. For of course she invited all the men of the world – except her father – to touch and imagine sucking. It was her revenge on his failure to be a father, whose principal psychoanalytic tasks are:

a) To protect the mother from the world, so she can breast-feed their child in peace.
b) To protect their child from her mother, so she can develop into a woman/mother.
c) To protect the child from herself, her unmanageable thoughts and emotions.
d) To protect the child from himself, his rage at being displaced by the child, and his desire that the child be his *pleasure-object*.

Lolo's avowed absence of desire to be seen and touched shows the terrifying levels of ambivalence that the Oedipal drama produces. Her mother, broken by *her own* mother, felt so humiliated by the public display and by her daughter's Monroesque drug-death that she displaced all her own sense of envy and guilt into a 'maternal' revenge-rage at her son-in-law.

Apart from the relational longings, there are of course the ordinary developmental tasks for the baby/child of attaining control of appetite and excretion – the mouth and the anal and urethral valves. Attending these are experiences of fullness, some-times satisfying and sometimes unbearable, and experiences of evacuation which waver between a sense of expulsion, escape and grief over loss. But from early on, there is another dimension to the baby/child's life: its ability to be concerned with neither food nor desire, but to concentrate on tasks that seem without purpose or meaning for survival or con-nection – play and art. Later, some teenagers and adults would rather spend all their free (required-work free) energy in play and making than in fucking or even eating.

Freud believed that there must be some mechanism at work which facilitates the ordinary management of these inchoate instincts and energies and also directs them into the channels of play and art. One of these is sublimation. The theory of instincts and their trans-formations underpins all psychoanalytic theory. In a common perception of instinctual forces, there are just two simple modalities – attraction and repulsion or, in the human realm, love and hate. Freud's major contribution was to suggest that the instincts of sexuality and aggression are far more protean and subtle than they appear even to the cold eye of adult misanthropy. It is not too fanciful to say that Freud wavered between a perception of himself as a poet of high metaphorical abstraction and as a hard-scientist, like Mendeleyev, who would present a complete periodic table of the elemental instincts which, in their connections and transformations, would account for human development. Perhaps he was also struck by the scientific meaning of sublimation: to pass from solid to gas without an intervening liquid state.

Let us begin with the more familiar and definitive kind of instinct.

a) My partner, out of curiosity and sorority, asked her brother-in-law to bring his doe rabbit to 'visit' our middle-aged buck, who had not seen another rabbit since we got him at birth. The moment the doe entered the room, he attempted to mount her. Alas, she was not receptive. (What, no dinner and small talk?) After she left, our poor lover was distressed for hours.

b) Place food in front of a hungry dog which is neither afraid nor being pleasantly distracted, and it will not defer troughing in order to play or make pretty patterns in the soil.

c) A friend once kept three dogs from birth. She observed that two would not eat until the 'top dog' had begun to eat. But when this dog was passed on to another friend, the remaining two became 'neurotic' about beginning to eat: they seemed to have no cue. They didn't outgrow this anxiety.[37]

It is an anthropomorphic fallacy to say that those two dogs were paralysed by some kind of introjected superego. But it is a different kind of species-fallacy to deny special meaning and consequence to the greater period of developmental dependency and the latency period in humans.

In addition to the long-known characteristics of urgency and latency, Freud broadened the conception of the sexual instinct by positing the characteristic of plasticity. The 'obvious' species aim of the sexual instinct is genital docking. But the copulating human couple's experience is significantly different from that of dogs and bunnies. It involves the excitation of non-genital parts of the body: the lips, tongue, anus, skin, the eyes (scopophilia, the desire to look), and the mind (epistemophilia, the desire to know). In normal development, the point of non-genital excitation is to provide a forepleasure which, though it might be pleasurable in itself, gets its value from providing the gathering of energy for the genital connection and its associated discharge of tension – physical and mental. The less obvious aim is asexual:

It [the sexual instinct] *places extraordinarily large amounts of force at the disposal of civilized activity, and it does this in virtue of its especially marked characteristic of being able to displace its aim without materially diminishing in intensity. This capacity to exchange its originally sexual aim for another one, which is no longer sexual but which is psychically related to the first aim, is called the capacity for sublimation.*[38]

Freud inferred from the non-genital aspects of adult sexuality the following developmental schema. The infant becomes aware of forms of excitation, tension and pleasurable relief, located in certain parts of the body. Unsurprisingly, these locii of superlative excitation are associated with the primary functions of feeding and excretion – the mouth and the anus/urethra. Both good and bad feeds and good and bad excretions provide the child with a sense of the range of pleasure and unpleasure. Interestingly, Freud suggested a third pre-genital stage after the oral and the anal: the phallic. This is a stage of mental/

24

conceptual excitation based on the infant/child's curiosity about its own body and the bodies of its carers. (It is not a mere envy or glorification of the penis.) This desire to see and to know meets the frustrations of two boundaries. Neither the inside of its own body nor that of its mother is visible. And, gradually, even parts of the external body of the mother are denied to sight. Accompanying this is the relinquishing by the child of its absolute and exclusive desire for its mother in favour of new forms of identity and relatedness; namely, the resolution of the Oedipus complex.

As well as achieving the mighty developmental tasks of weaning and excretion control, the child learns how to learn, work, play and be alone and with others. Manifestations by children of latency-period sexuality have an aim of stimulation of the child's own body, and the consequential pleasure, but do not yet have a sexual object, an Other. Thus the crucial distinction that children have sexual phantasies but not sexual fantasies: the former, mostly unconscious, are of their nature more relational and conceptually explorative than grossly physical.

Freud took these two data – the fact of this seemingly boundless yet unusable sexual instinctual energy, and the fact of the developmental tasks of learning to play, relate and work – and posited various mechanisms to connect them.

It is important to remember that Freud saw sublimation as a normal element in the development towards the adult goals of the ability to love and to work (including genital love and creative intelligence). Inadequate discharge, control and sublimation of the instinct leads to various pathologies:

1. Sexual perversion: fixation at varieties of pre-genital, namely non-genital, sexual fascination and discharge.
2. Sexual neuroses: non-sexual bodily discharge as physical symptoms/ailments. (In a brilliant aphorism, Freud connected these two pathologies – 'neuroses are the "negative" of the perversions' – and made the observation that in some 'civilized' families these pathologies are distributed by gender.[39])
3. Emotional disaffection: an inability to form and negotiate human relationships, not just as a lover or parent, but also as a friend or even a colleague.
4. Philistinism: the refusal of or abstinence from the creative impulse – not simply refusing to listen to opera or scorning museums. It also denies the worth of artistic criticism.

Freud's theory is a dynamic, economic and some would say typically 19th-century mechanical paradigm. But how else to describe the progress of a process? Let us ask ten basic questions:

1. WHICH instincts are involved in sublimation?

When Freud stated in a twilight lecture, 'The theory of the instincts is so to say our mythology',[40] he was not questioning their explanatory value, any more than Homer was when grappling with the fundamental concepts of humanity and divinity. Freud dissented from the common reflex to propose *ad hoc* instincts for any human experience or activity, e.g., assertion, gardening, macramé. He began with two instincts, sexuality and aggression, and moved towards the complementary pair, the life/self-preservative and death instincts – Eros and Thanatos. He rejected the existence of a social instinct, seeing self-identity and social-identity as developmental markers generated by the basic instincts. If these mythological entities are the conceptual sentinels for Freud, they play themselves out on the terrain of bodily sensation. The defining characteristics of an instinct, in this sense, are that it has a source, an aim and an object. The source is internal and inescapable bodily excitation, the aim is the discharge of excitation which is uncontainable, and the object is what facilitates, or is perceived to facilitate, the aim.

2. What can HAPPEN to instincts?

In order to present his fundamental belief in a permanent dynamic tension in and between human beings, Freud posited a permanent tension between the instincts. When the interactions between the instincts produce unbearable tensions, namely anxiety, then certain defence mechanisms come into play and the instincts undergo various transformations of aim and object. When attempting to describe the frustrations, renunciations, discharges, transformations and vicissitudes of instincts, he spoke of:

a) exchange
b) psychically related
c) mastering and deflecting
d) shifting
e) changed in the course of their growth
f) induced to displace
g) suppression, repression, reaction formation
h) reversal into its opposite
i) turning round upon the subject's own self
j) fusion and defusion
k) sublimation[41]

There is not space to give an account of all of these. The important point is that sublimation is a part of ordinary development and not a pathological defence.

3. What is the HEALTHY instinctual development?

Freud's account of development is invitingly simple and troublingly complex at the same time. The psychoanalytic terms for the agencies – *id*, *ego* and *superego* – and for the stages – 'oral', 'anal', 'phallic' and 'genital' – are as often used in ordinary conversation as rocket science's 'electrons' and 'black holes'. The complexity lies in his passing between these levels of explanation and in his change of emphasis and metaphor as he developed his theory. He suggests the metaphor of the id as a horse managed by the ego – but by using the 'borrowed forces' of the id, as if developmentally the rider grew out of the horse, like a centaur![42] The first axiom of the instinctual theory is that there is a great reservoir of undifferentiated instinctual energy, 'libido'; but this is variously called both the id and the ego. In restricting, for simplicity's sake, my account to the 1923 paper, *The Ego and the Id*, I am not denying the place of the variations.

The going-out or investment of a portion of that energy in an Object, Freud called 'cathexis'. For some thing, some Object, some person, to become knowable to consciousness, the mental presentation of that thing, the thing-presentation, has to be attached/connected to a word-presentation – an externally spoken but internally heard sensation. The puzzle is: could one express/articulate one's experience of the desire for, or satisfaction in, the Object *before* the connection was made – the pure affect?; or afterwards, the residue of affect that the word can't capture? This is a logical as well as developmental impossibility. Who can possibly *say* how much he, as a baby, wanted the breast or the sight of mummy?

When the sexual/libidinal instinct meets frustration, by the external object or internal anxiety, the cathexis is abandoned: the outgoing energy is drawn back by the id. It is desexualised and becomes the basis of the ego. 'The character of the ego is a precipitate of abandoned object-cathexes and it contains the history of those object-choices.'[43] Because the first interactions with the Object (carer) introduce the baby to the sense of the physical surface of its body as a boundary between it and the world, Freud spoke of the ego as 'first and foremost a bodily ego: it is not merely a surface entity, but is itself the projection of a surface'.[44]

There is a transitional phase, in which the inchoate

ego presents itself as an Object for the id, that Freud termed (secondary) narcissism. And here he made only a conjecture: 'The question arises, and deserves careful consideration, whether this is not *the universal road to sublimation*, whether all sublimation does not take place through the mediation of the ego, which begins by changing sexual object-libido into narcissistic libido and then, perhaps, goes on *to give it another aim*.'[45]

The resolution of the Oedipus complex, for baby boys, consists in the withdrawal of libidinal cathexis from the mother and an identification with the father. The introjection of paternal prohibition becomes the psychic entity, the superego. But the other consequence of 'the ego's work of sublimation' is 'a defusion of the instincts and a liberation of the aggressive instincts in the super-ego'.[46] In a chilling phrase, Freud describes the superego as 'a pure culture of the death instinct'.[47] When we consider that it is also the site of evaluation – ethics and aesthetics – we can understand why Freud thought of healthy development as merely a theoretical ideal.

The story is further complicated by the fact of the child's 'homosexual tendencies'. After the anaclitic (non-narcissistic) heterosexual object-choice, these 'combine with portions of the ego-instincts . . . and help to constitute the social instincts, thus contributing an erotic factor to friendship and comradeship, to *esprit de corps* and to the love of mankind in general'.[48] Friendship can be seen as a crucial mid-term of human connectivity between kinship and citizenship. But though we all have experiences of the subtle varieties of friendship, why are there so few terms for them? What is unthinkable here about the gradations of obligation and gratitude? Why is it so hard for this muted Eros to speak its many names?

Freud then makes the observation that it is chaste homosexuals, who have performed what I would call a secondary-level sublimation, who 'are distinguished by taking a particularly active share in the general interests of humanity'.[49] In his account of the life of the greatest chaste homosexual, Leonardo da Vinci, Freud conjectured that 'he succeeded in sublimating the greater part of his libido into an urge for research'.[50] It is more common for the instinct for research to be repressed along with the sexual instinct, or for thinking to become sexualised. But Freud still concluded that he had not explained this.

4. What is the DEFINING MECHANISM of sublimation?

The concise formula as given by Rycroft is: 'All

sublimations depend on symbolization and all ego development depends on sublimation.'[51] And symbolisation itself depends on the mechanisms of displacement and substitution (and condensation). There is the familiar reference point of symbolisation as a result of intra-psychic conflict, in which something bearable is made to stand for something still unbearable. This is an idea most easily understood in dream symbols, but still resisted with respect to physiological symptoms. But it still seems *a bridge too far*, or *a seventh degree of separation*, between the nipple and Nobel. And yet such bridges are being made all the time, from infancy.

Think of Freud's baby playing with his wooden reel and string. While his mother is away, invisible, he casts out and hauls back the reel, saying *'fort* [gone] . . . *da* [there]': the 'toy' *as* mother.[52] It was a lovely coincidence to find that when Elizabeth Gaskell's motherless heroine, Molly, is nine years old, she tells her father about her fantasy of having him on an unbreakable thread.[53] In the early case history, *Dora*, Freud saw transference as including 'revised editions' of earlier sublimations.[54] Think of the typically human propensity to seek similes and metaphors to communicate meaning – 'O, my love's like a red, red rose'[55] – and do not forget the long tradition of seeing the vagina as a rose, or even 'the mystic rose'. Think of Picasso showing bicycle handlebars *as* a bull's head. Psychoanalysts distinguish psychotics from neurotics by their lack of precisely this ability. Think of the childhood word-puzzles in which one word is to be turned into another, by changing one letter at a time. This strengthens the faculty of displacement even without symbolisation. Think of the uncanniness of some words having two opposite meanings, as Freud did with 'uncanny'![56] The therapeutic rule of free-association facilitates these incremental shifts, these tiny stepping stones across the roaring waters of the unconscious. Perhaps the analyst's task is to help the client make a Venice of her mind.

5. HOW MUCH sublimation is possible?

The original strength of the sexual instinct probably varies in each individual: certainly the proportion of it which is suitable for sublimation varies. It seems to us that it is the innate constitution of each individual which decides in the first instance how large a part of his sexual instinct it will be possible to sublimate and make use of. In addition to this, the effects of experience and the intellectual influences on his mental apparatus succeed in bringing about the sublimation of a further portion of it. To extend this process of displacement indefinitely is, however, certainly not possible, any more than is the case with the transformation of heat into mechanical energy in our machines. A certain amount of direct sexual satisfaction seems to be indispensable [to avoid neurotic illness].[57]

This suggests that there is what might be called 'innate primary sublimation' and a 'secondary sublimation' which rides on the benefits of the former. At the societal level, if there is too much 'civilised' sexual morality – namely, excessive legal and institutional constraint on forms and occasions of sexual expression – then citizens will not only not be able to love well and happily, but will also be unable to think and create the very inventions and objects that the community takes as indices of its civilisation: 'Neuroses, whatever their extent and wherever they occur, always succeed in frustrating the purposes of civilization.'[58]

6. WHEN is sublimation most possible?

'Sublimation . . . can be achieved only intermittently, and least easily during the period of ardent and vigorous youth.'[59] This negative definition suggests

35

that an individual's capacity for sublimation is shaped in latency. As Anna Freud observed, some ardent youths display an extraordinary relish for asceticism.[60] After that, even when desire outstrips ardent and vigorous ability, the pressure of mental desire – sex in the head – can be debilitating.

7. By WHOM is sublimation most possible?

'Sublimation can be achieved by a minority . . . Most of the rest become neurotic or are harmed in one way or another.'[61] Most people today would agree with Freud's scepticism about adolescent sublimation and his excoriation of the '"double" sexual morality for men', but they would be hesitant about the validity of the following observation: 'Experience shows as well that women, who, as being the actual vehicle of the sexual interests of mankind, are only endowed in a small measure with the gift of sublimating their instincts.'[62] We will pick up this theme later. When Freud states, 'An abstinent artist is hardly conceivable: but an abstinent young *savant* is certainly no rarity',[63] this seems to fit in with all of one's clichés of randy artists or 'sex and drugs and rock 'n' roll'. Apart from hypocrites like Stendhal's Julien Sorel, most adolescents would prefer to be Hesse's sensual Goldmund than the ascetic Narziss. Interestingly,

Freud himself was to provide, two years later in 1910, a stunning counter example of the abstinent creative genius (for he was as much a scientist as he was an artist) in his study of Leonardo.[64]

There seems to be an initial paradox. If artists experience the zenith of the capacity for sublimation, the perfect equilibrium between sexual instincts and creative expression, why do they seem to want so much sex, and often unsatisfying and cruel sex? Perhaps because even artists rarely experience equilibrium – in fact, the other cliché of the artist or scientist is that of one who is 'mad'. What disturbs their balance are other instincts, which we examine below.

8. Is sublimation possible in WORK, the day job?

Humans must sublimate in order to enjoy art or to be artists. This is the loosest summary of the theory. But where does this leave all of the other non-sexual activities, also facilitated by sublimation – all of the thinking and doing and making of things which are not intended to be art-objects? What happens at work, the nine-to-five? A discussion of 'the significance of work for the economics of the libido' was among the topics Freud left undeveloped.[65] When he writes that:

37

Professional activity is a source of special satisfaction if it is a freely chosen one – if, that is to say, by means of sublimation, it makes possible the use of existing inclinations, of persisting or constitutionally reinforced instinctual impulses . . .[66]

. . . he is really only redefining work as art. For most people, their limited creativity as well as external necessity and obligation mean that they endure rather than enjoy their jobs. One consequence of this is that their leisure time and their non-work relationships become the site of their more successful sublimations – or of the even more urgent expression of their sexual and other instincts.

9. Is sublimation SUFFICIENTLY CONVULSING?

For Freud, physical relief and physical pleasure are the prototype: 'the sating of crude and primary instinctual impulses [which] convulse our physical being'.[67] In his earlier paper of 1908 he even emphasises his point: 'The sexual behaviour of a human being often *lays down the pattern* for all his other modes of reacting to life.'[68] So the act of creation (artistic or scientific) and the aesthetic experience may be called 'finer and higher', but they are merely 'mildly intoxicating', inducing a 'mild narcosis'.[69] Similarly, Freud was sceptical of the comforting illusions of religion and the worth of spiritual/meditative bliss. This seems to be the realm of impossible comparison. Freud never advocated using another person as a kind of sexual toilet, and found it 'ethically objectionable' when sex became 'a convenient game'.[70] The Other is to be shared, not merely had, and only in the context of one offering oneself to be shared and not merely had. This is because our attainment of the reality principle is defined by our ability not merely to recognise the other, but also when necessary to wait for the other to recognise himself as himself and not simply as our construct. The possibly greater convulsions of careless sex would be of lower value because too much hatred of the Self and the Other remained unsublimated.

It is an ordinary experience to have shed more convulsive tears at a high tragedy on the stage than at the death of a dearkin – but still to feel the difference in value. One might imagine uniting two intensities, as did my philosophy tutor when he said: 'For me, the supreme pleasure would be to have sex and do higher maths at the same time.'[71] But first one must have a sense of their separate intensities. Being reminded of this, one soon realises the impossibility. Yet it is a developmental crux to arrive at that thought. It is fitting that a poet, Yeats, adumbrated the idea more elliptically:

The fascination of what's difficult
Has dried the sap out of my veins, and rent
Spontaneous joy and natural content
Out of my heart.[72]

Instinctual vein-coursing satisfaction is displaced by the mind's fascination with a puzzle. Some see this as one of the highest gifts that a teacher can induce in, or impart to, a pupil. Unlike Sting or Hindu adepts, I can't comment on the uniting of two other intensities, sex and spirituality, in Tantric practices. But I am struck by the way in which the experience of the force of creation has led, in many cultures, to the force being named and personified: *Muses* in Greek and European literature, *Ras* in Hinduism, *Duende* in Spanish, and *Mojo* (fetish?) in voodoo and rock culture. Is this force to be seen as the residue of sublimation, somehow out there now but still accessible? And are these the non-sexual correlates of the projections of incubi and succubi?

10.   What is the EVIDENCE for sublimation?

Psychoanalysis has been endlessly taunted for its lack of scientific proof. Even when it is stated that it provides explanation without prediction, this is still mocked as being insufficiently scientific. It is charged with committing the fallacy of affirming the consequent, and generally ignoring too much that it doesn't know. Freud's remark above about the vast energies of the sexual instinct, and the tendencies of all intense human emotions to find sexual expression, would probably be cited by his opponents as proof of his indefensible pan-sexualism. But consider these two stories, from playwrights:

a) A middle-aged woman, broken by grief at her father's death earlier that day, finds comfort and release in almost animalistically urgent, yet weeping, sex with her unreliable lover.[73]

b) A young English soldier gets an erection during a tour of a German death-camp.[74]

Here are two ordinary examples of absolute terror and absolute dismay finding sexual expression. Explain that without Freud! Even Kant would say that here was simply a lack of emotional resources to take comfort in the conceptual sublime itself – and the person therefore thrown back upon a bodily solution.

For sublimation, there are two basic types of evidence from therapeutic practice:

a) The client is enabled by analysis to discover the proper or deeper way to love and work, to relate to people and express her creativity. An analysis of her childhood inhibitions of sexual curiosity allows the belated completion of the necessary sublimations, which free up adult intellectual curiosity and expression.

b) The corollary is when someone who used to be able to love and work 'reasonably' well breaks down, after which he can barely do either. Again, the factor of an earlier imperfect sublimation can be seen when someone who had an inquiring mind regresses to the point of voyeurism and over-eating.[75]

Freud's rare incursion into child analysis also provides support for his thesis. After the five-year-old Hans had given up masturbation and looking at others on the toilet, his father observed that 'simultaneously with this repression a certain amount of sublimation set in':

From the time of the beginning of his anxiety Hans began to show an increased interest in music and to develop his inherited musical gift.[76]

'Hans' grew up to be Herbert Graf, the opera singer and visually innovative director at the New York Met.[77]

Finally, it is important to state Freud's hesitation:

Instincts and their transformations are at the limit of what is discernible by psychoanalysis. From that point it gives place to biological research.[78]

Mindin' i&i Own Business: Other Psychoanalytic Contributions

It was Freud's children, literal and metaphorical, who undertook the analysis of children. Unsurprisingly, he believed that their research would confirm his theories. So now we move across the teens. Puberty is fundamentally a biological reorganisation. For some boys, this sudden explosion of hormones seems to deprive them of the ability even to walk properly; they slope or even stumble, not quite knowing the extremities of their own body – Harry Enfield's comic adolescent character, Kevin, shows this perfectly. I am reminded again of Freud's remark about the ego

43

as a bodily ego. All teenagers like their music played loud. Many boys like a kind of noise which is barely music – heavy metal – played uncomfortably loud. Interestingly, this musically aggressive genre is known as 'cock-rock'. (I hope it's obvious why.) My conjecture about the predilection for loud music is that it is a way of meeting and defeating the 'voices' of the superego.

Before latency, the child knew that its Oedipal desires were frustrated by incapacity – a tiny penis, no breasts. But now that ability can put desire into effect, the only inhibitions are morality and the traces or echoes of former terror of parental revenge. Does throwing oneself into the mosh-pit symbolically re-enact the adolescent desire to re-enter the womb? It was said that the predominance of nappy-pins in punk dress showed an ambivalence about being grown-up. Their inclusion of the swastika was the most pitifully puerile and apolitical element in their rage against the parental love-generation. In *The Buddha of Suburbia*, the mother pleads with her son: 'Please take off the swastika. I don't care about anything else.'[79]

There is also the ordinary cross-cultural fact that first love makes poets of all adolescents. Why should there be such a new aesthetic sensitivity to nature and a compulsion to fashion words into form? It is usually bad poetry, but this equation of sexual urgency, emotional longing and aesthetic fascination indicates a second flowering of sublimation.

I will look at two great theorists of childhood.

1. Melanie Klein

Klein took Freudian theory into the nursery, across the realm of words into the gestures and toys that are the symbolic pre-verbal language of children. From her observations of children at play, she concluded that Oedipal conflicts trouble the child long before the age at which Freud placed them. And of course at that age the child is at the mercy of instincts and emotions he can barely manage, let alone name. Klein is equal to Freud in producing 'shocking' aphorisms: 'the *school*-task signifies coitus or masturbation'; 'athletic games of every sort have a libidinal cathexis and genital symbolism'.[80] Consider this case material:

For [almost seven-year-old] *Fritz, when he was* writing, *the lines meant roads and the letters rode on motorcycles – on the pen – upon them. For instance 'i' and 'e' ride together on a motorbicycle that is usually driven by the 'i' and they love one another with a tenderness quite unknown in the real world . . . The 'l's' are represented as stupid, clumsy, lazy and dirty. They live in caves under the earth.*[81]

Klein arrives, via the child's associations, at the interpretation that 'i' is the penis and 'l' faeces. But even if one baulked at that, there is something to be explained about the child's expenditure of energy in the narrative construction, classification and evaluation of the letters – things are being connected, displaced, symbolised. (One of the things I remember most clearly about the trip in my youth, when I passed chemically through the doors of perception, was a 'brief' episode in which the visible manifold seemed to have a transparent veneer of hundreds of brightly coloured capital letters.) It is hard for an adult to remember the impact of written letters on the construction and meaning of reality. When it comes to remembering the impact of the first words heard, we are lost. Perhaps it is an attempt to recapture these first sensations which prompts my friend's eight-year-old daughter Lisa to insist that the words her father reads to her at bedtime are words she *can't* understand.

Klein refers to H. Sperber, who had argued that 'sexual impulses have played an important part in the evolution of speech'; mating calls developed 'as a rhythmic accompaniment to work, which thus became associated with sexual pleasure'.[82] And she followed Sándor Ferenczi in positing a stage of identification before the stage of symbolisation. He had observed that 'at an early stage of its development the child tries to rediscover its bodily organs and their activities in every object which it encounters. Since it institutes a similar comparison with its own body as well, it probably sees in the upper part of its body an equivalent for each *affectively important* detail of the lower part.'[83] It is this limiting case of comparison which facilitates the beginning of symbolisation and future sublimation.

The Oedipal conflict in which the child, formed of masculine and feminine components, has both heterosexual and homosexual longings, is resolved differently by boys than by girls. Klein went on to assert that:

The contribution which the feminine component makes to sublimation will probably always prove to be receptivity and understanding, which are an important part of all activities: the driving executive part, however, which really constitutes the character of any activity, originates in the sublimation of masculine potency.[84]

She used this to explain the fact that in her generation (and all previous ones) girls did better than boys at school, but not later on. This very year, research is published that shows girls continuing to do better than boys at university. So, even political solutions such as better access to college can attenuate a girl's castration complex – *her* version of *every* child's anxiety about an insufficiency of means – and facilitate sublimation and creativity.

We saw above how children can expend considerable amounts of (libidinal) energy on the minutest elements of literacy and oracy. Unsurprisingly, this barely bounded energy continues to be a part of the process of learning. Ordinary conversation reveals multifarious metaphors connecting food and digestion with reading and writing – the *voracious* reader, the *stodgy* book. In a brilliant paper, 'Some Unconscious Factors in Reading', James Strachey suggests that the way in which a person negotiates the two oral phases – sucking and biting – influences their later emotional tone towards reading and writing. The equally ordinary fact of many people enjoying reading while shitting, he suggests, contains a 'symbolic act of coprophagy'.[85] If this strikes the reader as too wild, he would do well to ponder, like Strachey, on the Word of God through Ezekiel:

And thou shalt eat [thy meat] *as barley cakes and thou shalt bake it with dung that cometh out of man, in their sight. Therefore the fathers shall eat the sons in the midst of thee and the sons shall eat their fathers.*[86]

A more benign equation of reading and eating can be seen in a medieval Jewish ritual. Scriptural extracts would be written on eggs or cakes or a slate, then covered with honey. The young initiate would be asked to read to the teacher, and then be invited to lick and eat.[87] This appetitive connection is maintained in Proverbs: 'The lips of a strange woman drop as an honeycomb'[88] – which of course translates in male fantasy, bloke-speak, as the stunner on the train suddenly saying: 'Eat me, big boy!'

As the child moves from mere letters and words to intentional meaning, some of his slips in reading and writing and speaking assume the pathology of unconscious meaning. In their *On Learning to Read*, Bruno Bettelheim and Karen Zelan show how a child's 'academic' difficulties with literacy might have their roots in unconscious conflict.[89] Bettelheim alone, in the wonderfully entitled *The Uses of Enchantment*, had described the way in which children use fairy stories, with their themes of monsters and mutability, to process the conflicts of

49

ordinary development.[90] Why do children ask for a particular fairy story to be read again and again, without alteration? By this point, any kind of narrative surprise has long been exhausted. The reason is that elements of the story resonate with, and thereby rearrange, material in the child's unconscious. The story becomes a temporary container for that unmanageable material. It is as if the child waits for an emotional *Gestalt* switch which will indicate that the material has become manageable. That the process is sub-rational is shown by the very use of the word 'enchantment'. Perhaps the quality of the sublimation achieved is gauged by the child's ability to become the teller of that story to someone else – in other words, a young dramatic artist herself.

Klein believed that the creative impulse is grounded in the reparative impulse which marks the attainment of the depressive position – the stage when the child's anxiety that its aggressive thoughts and feelings towards its carer might have damaged her/him, prompt it to act to help, heal and attempt reconciliation.

2. Donald Winnicott

While accepting the received account of the sublimation of instinct, Winnicott felt that the theory needed developing in order to explain the phenomena revealed in his staggeringly large number of clinical observations of babies and children. 'Playing', he felt, 'needs to be studied as a subject on its own, supplementary to the concept of the sublimation of instinct'.[91] He proposed that in the maturational process facilitated by the 'good-enough mother', which takes a baby from a sense of me-as-the-whole-world to me-relating-to-a-not-me – that is, (my) mother, other people, objects – there is an intermediate position, an experiential space, a 'potential space', a third reality separable from inner reality and external reality. This is the realm of play and culture, and the 'objects' created/experienced here he calls 'transitional objects'. In trying to delineate this realm he is, perhaps, like Freud attempting his topography, drawn into paradoxical descriptions. For neither the baby's thumb nor its actual teddy bear is a transitional object. And yet, the transitional object is 'the child's first use of a symbol and the first experience of play'[92] – the beginning of language and culture.

Winnicott's greatest difference from Freud can be seen in his assertion that:

If when a child is playing the physical excitement of instinctual involvement becomes evident, then the playing stops, or is at any rate spoiled ... Play is immensely exciting, not primarily because the instincts are involved [but because of] *the precariousness of the interplay of personal psychic reality and the experience of control of actual objects ... There are significant mechanisms for object relating that are not drive-determined.*[93]

It is difficult to gauge here the way in which the instinctual forces which might provide the energy for play are held in abeyance to facilitate it.

Winnicott gives an example which bears an uncanny resemblance to the heroic *fort–da* baby. One of his young patients was a seven-year-old boy who was obsessed with string, playing with it, drawing it, even tying furniture together. This behaviour stopped when his mother articulated for him his memories and anxieties about separation. But even this could be called 'unpure' playing, laden as it is with a solution to a problem. Winnicott makes an important distinction between daydream-fantasising, which has no poetic value, and ordinary dreaming, which does. He refers to the look of a child playing – in its 'preoccupation ... it inhabits an area that cannot be easily left, nor can it easily admit intrusions'.[94]

The inability to play is for Winnicott a diagnostic

marker – both for adults and children. He was sceptical of the worth of intellectual interpretations, even for adults. The reparative experience that the psychoanalyst hopes to facilitate is 'of a non-purposive state . . . a sort of ticking over of the unintegrated personality',[95] a necessary experience of *being* if subsequent *doing* is to be genuinely creative and not merely compliant. I am reminded of Kant's description of the aesthetic state. The baby with the good-enough mother seems to have the aesthetic experience before it has attained to recognising aesthetic objects. This is also the conclusion of Christopher Bollas:

The aesthetic experience is not something learned by the adult, it is an existential recollection of an experience where being handled by the maternal aesthetic made thinking seemingly irrelevant to survival.[96]

Lipstick as Your Collar: Do Women Sublimate Differently?

[Suddenly, a surprise delivery of lipsticks.] *There were not enough of them to go round and here they were kicking and pummelling each other in order to possess*

one stick or even one of the right colour. It made me
feel sick to see them fighting . . .[97]

If you were told that this group was a bunch of fourth-formers, you might think: 'Ahh! the raging serious-ness of maiden-youth.' If it wasn't them, but a bunch of ravers at Studio 54, you might think: 'Spoilt bitches!' But if it was, and it was, Auschwitz, how would you begin to explain and even theorise this aggression? Who could say, who would be allowed to say? Only women, or even a man? In this section I will look at this puzzle and what it tells us about female sublimation.

It seems that there is a force almost as strong as the instinct for food and self-preservation, a force that can even ride the aggressive instinct in order to be satisfied. But what force or instinct – for protection, sexual signalling, for adornment or beauty? Some ethologists would remind us of the exposed, saturation-pink genitalia of chimps – so in-your-face that they obviously don't need Colour Endure – and conclude that the lipstick highlights the connection between the visible and the hidden orifices of pleasure and procreation. Does this mean that lipstick's verbal correlate is a kind of Jungle-Jane bush-telegraphese – 'Me cunt. You want?' Is this a self-objectification or a self-instantiation, or only the false Self of false-consciousness? If the object that a person makes into a thing of beauty and a joy for six hedonistic hours is oneself, is that sublimation? Even after three generations of feminism, a troubled mother can write to *The Times* Parent Forum: 'Is eight too young for make-up?'[98]

This is the realm of perilous controversy where sociology and politics cross swords with biology and psychoanalysis. How is a woman *marked* as a woman; how by herself and how by others? What does lipstick signify; what kind of alphabet do young girls find in their mother's make-up bags? In so brief a text, I can only point to some female perspectives.

The received generalisations of feminism begin with a castigation of the patriarchal legacy. 'Beauty is permanent injustice ... The man issues the law which will lock the woman away ... Freud figures as Public Enemy No. 1 ... analytic vocabulary more or less leaves out women altogether'.[99] Women interiorise these 'truths' and within a few generations there is 'misogyny – a crop sown by one woman and reaped by another'.[100] (cf. 'A bayonet is a weapon with a worker at each end.'[101]). These quotations come from Christiane Olivier's polemic *Jocasta's Children*. She, too, begins with the mighty Sophoclean tale of

Oedipus, but asks why 'it never seems to occur to them [women] to think to themselves, even for a moment, "I'm going through my Jocasta stage"'.[102]

In foregrounding Jocasta, Olivier reminds us of the fact of the mother's sexual desire for her baby. This spectrum of desire has at one pole the absolute perversion of actually fucking the baby, and at the other the semi-mystical 'primary maternal pre-occupation' of Winnicott. In the middle band, there is mostly unconscious sexual desire resonating with the more accessible oral desire – the ordinary experience of finding one's dimpled baby nice enough to eat. But 'it is in her son', writes Olivier, 'that the mother has her only chance of seeing herself in male form'.[103] They form a mutually fascinated couple, and the problem for the boy is one of degrees of fusion and abandonment. In Olivier's formulation, the girl-child never attains to such libidinous mutuality.

The stark fact [is] that the girl has no primary love-object . . . daughters come through a relationship with their mother that had no desire in it, and then, more or less belatedly, switched to their father.[104]

A boy sees his anatomy writ large in his father. Whereas 'it is not uncommon to see a little girl first touching her mother's breasts and then her own chest and saying "Katie no boobs'",[105] few if any mothers point to the similarity of the possession of a clitoris. So 'the mother cannot be a locus of identification for the girl'.[106]

This early awareness of her insufficiency as a woman and as a desired object gives a girl a lifelong burden of proof of womanliness and desirability, a legacy of forever making-up to look other than the naked Self. The reparative paternal gaze is usually insufficient, because the father must be at work or is still trying to escape his own mother, seen behind the façade of his wife. So the absence of a sufficient gaze from both mother and father leaves the girl doomed to feeling unseen. If the solution is 'I attract, therefore I am', then is the struggle 'Am I or am I not to put on the colour "woman"?'[107] (cf. Jean Genet's dramatic premise that in a racist society, non-whites must put on and play the colour 'black'.[108]) To please is the default-setting learned by girls.

If the datum of vast libidinal energy in children is gender blind, the obvious question is: what are the consequences for the girl-child whose libido is not discharged by maternal desire, nor by the paternal gaze? Freud argued for a weaker capacity for sublimation in women. Perhaps because his client base was different, he failed to see that 'sublimation is *incredibly present and active* in the life of little girls: girls draw better, write better poems, make up far livelier plays than boys'.[109] At puberty, this development is thwarted by sociology, not biology. The structure that men make in order to facilitate adult sexuality, maternity and child rearing, results in her potential for sublimation being vitiated. In Olivier's rhetorical flourish: 'Man snatches sublimation away from woman by loading children onto her ... they are shut away in their bodies.'[110] Men do this 'so as not to have to meet [women] in the ground of sublimation'.[111]

Anorexics defend against the need for the male gaze by stalling the development of their bodies, and they often remain absorbed by high intellectual attainment – thus asserting the right to continuing sublimation. Another strategy of the sublimating woman who attains Parnassus (or Yale) is, as first-generation analyst Joan Riviere observed, to 'put on a mask of womanliness to avert anxiety and retribution feared from men'.[112] The most tragic choice is that taken by Claire Marsh, whose aspiration to gain male notice by appropriating masculinity – to be a 'laddette' or 'geezer girl' – sank to its nadir this year when she became, at 18, the youngest woman ever to be convicted of rape.[113]

And in married life, the disparity grinds on. The home that a 'virtuous wife' creates allows the man – who has been fighting the world outside – to regress, to be a child, to eat and to read and to play in his den. But who creates such a space for her? How many women can trust their partners to be a good-enough parent for their young kids for a few hours? 'Once regression has been lost to them they find themselves without sublimation. [This] is the missing sector in the lives of women and mothers.'[114] I will return to these psycho-political themes below.

Francette Pacteau takes up a similar position: 'No man escapes castration anxiety . . . no woman escapes "beauty".'[115] From the male point of view, 'formulations of feminine beauty by men appear to be largely unconscious, indeed unconsciously motivated. They correspond to a variety of (mainly) masculine symptoms.'[116] In her study, *The Symptom of Beauty*, Pacteau focuses on the way in which beauty is attributed to women, the way the fantasy stages – creates the *mise-en-scène* for – this symptom. From the female side, 'there is, always, the image to which the question of her beauty must be referred. As beautiful as . . . .'.[117] Madonna wanted to be a 'better' Monroe than Blondie managed. But what did Marilyn's model want . . .? Interestingly, the pervasiveness of their images means that none of these photo and film idols attains the aura of the *concept*, the *structural ideal*, that takes the imagination to the limit, e.g., 'The face that launched a thousand ships', or 'The love of the man of seven hundred wives', as in Helen of Troy and the Shulamite of Jerusalem.[118]

Pacteau takes from Anzieu his idea of 'skin ego', a development of Freud's basic idea of the bodily ego.[119] Initially, the infant has no sense of separation of skin or the direction of touch. Weaning and socialisation are defined by the incremental prohibitions on touching, at first the mother's body and then one's own. For the boy, it is the line against incest; for the girl, the line of ambivalent rejection – for although girls are weaned earlier, yet they may touch the mother for longer. Touching is sublimated into looking: contact-perception is replaced by distance-perception. The child copes with the seduction and aggression inherent in the prohibitions by creating the fantasy of a second skin as impenetrable and protective as the mother's skin. This thought induces the anxiety that the mother could and might tear off and repossess one's own skin. It is the girl's greater anxiety to *inhabit* visibility and to attract desire (or at least gazing) that leads to her greater

fascination with the permutations of second skin –
clothes, fabrics and furs, and the panoply of make-up.
Men are of course fascinated by the revelation of skin,
from ankles to cleavage to tights-tops . . . Yet when a
man finally gets to the skin, he first meets his anxiety
about the surface of his mother.

Sublimation was defined above as a substitution of
non-sexual aims and objects for sexual ones, allowing
for a mastery of both sexual and non-sexual objects.
But, interestingly, in the cultural domain of fine art –
painting and sculpture – the sublimating artist is
preoccupied with the body as sexual object. 'The self-
portrait of the artist at work', writes Pacteau, 'we may
now read as a *mise-en-scène* of sublimation'.[120] So
how to read the painting, 'The Origin of Drawing'?
This is based on the legend in which a young woman
draws the outline of the shadow cast on a wall by her
beloved. One thinks of the possible refractions of the
Freudian phrase, 'the shadow of the object fell upon
the ego',[121] and wonders about this legend choosing
a female artist. Pacteau continues by arguing that
one of the ways of mastering the excess sexual energy
in this creating experience, and of the body in general,
is to intellectualise it – the rules of proportion for
the body and for perspective in the artwork. 'The
mathematization of the "well-proportioned" body

offers a privileged instance of sublimation.'[122] Another way to master is by *fragment* and *concept* – for example, the medieval 'blasons', poems on bits of the body, or Courbet offering a headless, footless woman with the vagina at vanishing point, and not calling it 'Con' but 'The Origin of the World'.

In the work of the conceptual artist Orlan we see a more literal destruction of perspective. She films herself directing others (doctors) tearing off her face to demonstrate the emptiness of the image. This strikes me as jejune and mad naïve realism, differently tragic from Lolo. Early socialists hoped for the withering away of state in the ideal of perfect civil society. If lipstick is an impression only for the Object, do feminists dream of the withering away of that second skin of make-up? But if it also carries a woman's potential for impressing/painting on the Object, the lover's lips or collar, what then? Will a feminist ever write a Milneresque tract: 'On Not Being Able to Not-paint One's Lips'?[123]

Foundationed Deep, Somehow: Psycho-Political Sublimation

We saw above how aesthetics places the emotions of desire, fear and anxiety within the framework of the conceptualisation of the ideas of form and limit, and how psychoanalysis argues for a transformation of desire and aggression, as well as anxiety, through sublimation. Our discussion has been focused on the individual and the family. In this closing section I want to look at the broader human connectivity – the *polis* – through two concepts, and ask what it means that the attempt to think about them seems to take us to the limit of our capacity for sublimation.

1. Genocide

Winnicott believed that it was possible to describe the conditions of good-enough parenting that might take the infant from kinship to democratic citizenship, and that might avoid the formation of a personality that needed the compensations of structural inequality or dictatorial and inegalitarian regimes, whether as master or slave.[124]

We might say that genocide is the (negative) political sublime, not merely disenfranchising a portion of the citizenry but 'deleting' it, by murder, from the register. How much imagination and perspective must one have to understand the fact of genocide? Even a scholar like Inga Clendinnen, with a deep knowledge of Aztec bloodlust, felt her imagination faint at the German Holocaust[125] – as did mine when I visited Auschwitz, and again on reading Tadeusz

Borowski's *This Way for the Gas, Ladies and Gentlemen*.[126] Claude Lanzmann, the documentary artist of *Shoah*, asserts the

. . . absolute obscenity in the very project of understanding. Not to understand was my iron law during all the eleven years of the production of Shoah. *I clung to this refusal of understanding as the only possible ethical and at the same time the only possible operative attitude. This blindness was for me the vital condition of creation.*[127]

Was Lanzmann attempting a rare fusion of sublimation and repression? The category of 'obscenity' reflects an abiding puzzlement of the fusion of sexuality and art. Herbert Marcuse coined the phrase 'repressive desublimation' for the use by the State of a relaxation of legal constraints on censorship and sexual expression that would be politically pacifying.[128] It might be thought that apostasy is merely benign unrepressive desublimation, but the State-faith readily interprets such psychologically freed-up 'new thinking' as fatal heresy. Interestingly, Jacques Lacan, working at the limits of understanding in the psychoanalytic domain, also took it as a rule 'that it is on the basis of a certain refusal of understanding that we open the door onto psychoanalytic under-standing'.[129]

By instituting National Holocaust Memorial Day, the present UK government set down an indication of the line of understanding for future children. But where was the space for scepticism about the project? For, tragically, the State understanding of genocide seems to include too much splitting: 'It was *them*, long ago. It couldn't happen *here*.' For me, the absolute filter is Walter Benjamin's eighth essay in his *Theses on the Philosophy of History*, written shortly before his suicide in 1940: 'The current amazement that the things we are experiencing are "still" possible in the twentieth century is not philosophical. This amazement is not the beginning of knowledge – unless it is the knowledge that the view of history which gives rise to it is untenable.'[130]

Of course, political history must reveal economic history. Interestingly, Freud's instinct-theory is often criticised for relying on a supposedly untenable analogy with economics, as well as mechanics. Perhaps this reveals an anxiety about placing the 'hidden hand' of economics. One can't run an empire – Roman, British, Nazi or American – without murder, extortion and neglect, nor without the co-operation of opportunist businessmen *far away* who want to *look* as if their hands are clean. The German Holocaust was unprecedented because the combination of State command economy and industrial possibility was unprecedented. As Edwin Black, author of the newly published *IBM and the Holocaust*, puts it: 'For the first time in history, an anti-Semite had automation on his side.'[131] We are left with the grim conclusion that human genocidal intention and the inertia of bystanders are a constant. How ought one to live with this thought? Is this the limit of psycho-political sublimation – transmuting hate into bureaucracy?

2. Maternity

Do not rush this next puzzle. Why can't you name one country or group of human beings, in ten millennia, that has taken as its *primary* criterion of civilisation, maternity – the absolute, unconditional, (free) provision of support for mother and child from conception to age five, and the mother's right to choose abortion, midwifery, maternity hospitals, childcare? It is shocking to read in *A History of Women's Bodies* by Edward Shorter that it is only in the past three generations, and then only in the West, that there has been sufficient care for the first year[132] – and not even that really: there remains a shortage of midwives and nurseries in the UK.

If 'Arbeit macht frei'[133] is *the* sick joke of the 20th century, then Genesis 3:16 is the nadir of five millennia of misogyny: 'Unto the woman He said, I will greatly multiply thy sorrow and thy conception: in sorrow thou shalt bring forth children.' If God was going to punish mortals with a pain in the gonads, then why not both sexes? Some say that this verse is the primary justification for the absence of sufficient maternity provision. The fact that non-Judaeo-Christian cultures have been equally careless – consider Indian society, where opportunist medics with mobile scanners help women to abort girls – reminds one that the problem is more to do with men and women as such: male rage at abandonment by the mother and male fear of fusion with the mother. The Nazi *Freikorps* who saw themselves as the peak of new German manhood positioned their own women as cold angels and the newly politicised Soviet women as hot demonic whores: both fantasies expressing fear and rage at frustrated desire. Their primary love-object was often their boyhood horse![134]

Two defining human characteristics are the absolute vulnerability of the child (and mother) at birth, and the ability to plan. Whatever economic or religious reasons there are and have been, the point is to think of the psychological reasons for this abiding indifference to mothers and children. Imagine *Mrs* Thatcher seeing the particularity of women. Imagine the Tories freeing mothers from *Miss* Widdecombe's chains. Imagine Tony Blair valorising 'maternity, maternity, maternity'. Imagine the Queen insisting to a cross-party committee that the millennium be marked by the creation, at Greenwich, in a bellied dome, of the best 'Museum and Research Centre of Maternity' in the world. And think why it remains so unthinkable. Two millennia of patriarchal Mariolatry do not atone for the billions of hours that women have spent with the terrifying thought: 'Am I late?' Is this another limit of psycho-political sublimation – transmuting biology into art, the poor revenge of men who can make rockets, icons and symphonies but who cannot *create* the ultimate object – a new human being?

Thinking's Gonna Change My World: Coda

The Greek word *metanoia* means 'change' and also 'redemption'. In the art of being human, the only sublimation worth talking about is that towards the moral sublime. The rest is mere *Sensation*. That which we *can't* think about – be it genocide, maternity, friendship – diminishes our humanity. We do well to recall that Primo Levi's poem *If This Is A Man* carries a conditional curse upon the unthinking reader: 'May your children turn their faces from you.'[135] Right now, a child is falling in the rye. Who is to catch it? If you try, then you will be among the sublimating élite – not drowning, but saving.[136]

Notes

References to Freud are given by paper title and date, and then: PFL = Penguin Freud Library (London: Penguin Books) with vol. no. and page ref.; SE = Standard Edition (London: Hogarth Press) with vol. no. and page ref.

1. Blake, W., *Selected Poems*, London: Penguin, 1988, p. 70.

2. Freud, S., 'The Uncanny' (1919), PFL 14, p. 368; SE 17, p. 245; *Civilization and Its Discontents* (1930), PFL 12, p. 271; SE 21, p. 83.

3. Woolf, V., *Orlando* (1928), London: Penguin, 1993, p. 100.

4. Manguel, A., *A History of Reading*, Canada: Vintage, 1996, p. 272.

5. Shakespeare, W., *Twelfth Night* (1601–2), I.i.1.

6. Keats, J., *Selected Poems*, London: Penguin, 1988, p. 89.

7. Tynan, K., *Profiles*, London: Nick Hern, 1990, p. 220.

8. Christiansen, R., *Romantic Affinities*, London: Vintage, 1994, p. 231.

9. Hare, D., *Teeth 'N' Smiles*, London: Faber and Faber, 1976; BBC2 Arts Night, September 1975.

10. Storr, A., book review of Shephard, B., *A War of Nerves*, London: Jonathan Cape, 2000, in *The Times*, London: 8 November 2000.

11. Apocryphal – various versions exist.

12. Riviere, J., 'Womanliness as a Masquerade', *International Journal of Psycho-Analysis*, vol. 10, 1929, p. 307.

13. Anderson, P.T., *Boogie Nights*, USA: 1999.

14. Turner, B. and Turner, T., *Third Rock From the Sun*, USA: 1997.

15. Shakespeare, W., *Hamlet* (1600–1), III.ii.117.

16. Kant, I., *The Critique of Judgement* (1790), trans. J. Meredith, Oxford: Oxford University Press, 1952, pp. 39, 58.

17. Ibid., p. 46.

18. Keats, J., letter (21 December 1817), in Gittings, R. (ed.), *Letters*, Oxford: Oxford University Press, 1970.

19. Bion, W., 'Notes on Memory and Desire', in Bott Spillius, E. (ed.), *Melanie Klein Today*, London: Routledge, 1988, pp. 17–21.

20. Kant (1952), op. cit., p. 107.

21. Ibid., p. 107.

22. Ibid., p. 106.

23. Ibid., pp. 91, 116.

24. Ibid., pp. 179, 210, 212.

25. Ibid., p. 223.

26. Ibid., pp. 49, 50, 191.

27. Plato, *The Republic* (c. 375 BC), London: Penguin, 1955.

28. Plato, *The Laws* (before 347 BC), London: Penguin, 1970.

29. Wind, E., *Art and Anarchy*, London: Duckworth, 1985, p. 94.

30. Lap-Chuen, T., *The Sublime*, Rochester, NY: University of Rochester Press, 1998.

31. Shandling, G., *The Larry Sanders Show*, USA: 1993.

32. Sondheim, S., *Profile* interview, *The Guardian*, London: 9 December 2000.

33. *Look at Lolo*, Channel 4 TV broadcast, London: 9 December 2000.

34. Goldman, A., *The Lives of John Lennon*, London: Bantam, 1988, pp. 246, 376, 470.

35. Gibson, I., *The Shameful Life of Salvador Dalí*, London: Faber and Faber, 1998, p. 165.

36. *Look at Lolo*, ibid.

37. Haynes, J. and Western, J., private conversation.

38. Freud, S., 'Civilized Sexual Morality' (1908), PFL 12, p. 39; SE 9, p. 187.

39. Ibid., PFL 12, p. 43; SE 9, p. 191.

40. Freud, S., *New Introductory Lectures* (1933), PFL 2, p. 127; SE 22, p. 95.

41. a)–c): Freud (1908), op. cit., PFL 12, pp. 39, 46; SE 9, p. 195; d)–g): Freud (1930), op. cit., PFL 12, pp. 267, 286; SE 21, p. 97; h)–k): Freud, S., *Instincts and Their Vicissitudes* (1915), PFL 11, p. 123; SE 14, p. 126.

42. Freud, S., *The Ego and the Id* (1923), PFL 11, p. 364; SE 19, p. 25.

43. Ibid., PFL 11, p. 368; SE 19, p. 29.

44. Ibid., PFL 11, p. 364; SE 19, p. 26.

45. Ibid., PFL 11, p. 369; SE 19, p. 30 (my emphasis).

46. Ibid., PFL 11, p. 398; SE 19, p. 56.

47. Ibid., PFL 11, p. 394; SE 19, p. 53.

48. Freud, S., *Schreber* (1911), PFL 9, pp. 198–9; SE 12, p. 61.

49. Ibid., PFL 9, p. 199; SE 12, p. 61.

50. Freud, S., *Leonardo* (1910), PFL 14, pp. 170–1; SE 11, p. 80.

51. Rycroft, C., *Dictionary of Psychoanalysis*, London: Penguin, 1968, p. 159.

52. Freud, S., *Beyond the Pleasure Principle* (1920), PFL 11, p. 284; SE 18, p. 15.

53. Gaskell, E., *Wives and Daughters* (1866), London: Penguin, 1996.

54. Freud, S., *Dora* (1905), PFL 8, p. 158; SE 7, p. 116.

55. Burns, R., *Selected Poems*, London: Penguin, 1996, p. 252.

56. Freud (1919), op. cit., PFL 14, p. 347; SE 17, p. 224.

57. Freud (1908), op. cit., PFL 12, pp. 39–40; SE 9, p. 188.

58. Ibid., PFL 12, p. 54; SE 9, p. 202.

59. Ibid., PFL 12, p. 45; SE 9, p. 193.

60. Freud, A., 'Adolescence' (1958), in *Anna Freud: Writings*, vol. 5, Madison, CT: International Universities Press, 1969.

61. Freud (1908), op. cit., PFL 12, p. 45; SE 9, p. 193.

62. Ibid., PFL 12, p. 47; SE 9, p. 195.

63. Ibid., PFL 12, p. 48; SE 9, p. 197.

64. Freud (1910), op. cit., PFL 14; SE 11.

65. Freud (1930), op. cit., PFL 12, p. 268fn; SE 21, p. 80fn.

66. Ibid., PFL 12, p. 268fn; SE 21, p. 80fn.

67. Ibid., PFL 12, p. 267; SE 21, p. 79.

68. Freud (1908), op. cit., PFL 12, p. 50; SE 9, p. 198.

69. Freud (1930), op. cit., PFL 12, pp. 267, 269, 271; SE 21, p. 81.

70. Freud (1908), op. cit., PFL 12, p. 52; SE 9, p. 200.

71. Black, B., private conversation.

72. Yeats, W.B., *Selected Poems*, London: Penguin, 2000, p. 66.

73. Hare, D., *The Secret Rapture*, London: Faber and Faber, 1997.

74. Griffiths, T., *Comedians*, London: Faber and Faber, 1976, p. 65.

75. Rycroft (1968), op. cit., p. 159.

76. Freud, S., *Little Hans* (1909), PFL 8, p. 295; SE 10, p. 138fn.

77. Norman, J., 'Little Hans', in Matthis, I. (ed.), *On Freud's Couch*, London: Jason Aronson, 1998, p. 94.

78. Freud (1910), op. cit., PFL 14, p. 229; SE 11, p. 136.

79. Kureishi, H., *The Buddha of Suburbia*, London: Faber and Faber, 1990.

80. Klein, M., *The School in Libidinal Development*

(1923a), and *Early Analysis* (1923b), in *Love, Guilt and Reparation and Other Works 1921–45*, London: Vintage, 1988, pp. 63, 77.

81. Klein (1923a), op. cit., p. 64.

82. Klein (1923b), op. cit., p. 85.

83. Ibid., p. 85 (my emphasis).

84. Klein (1923a), op. cit., p. 74 (my emphasis).

85. Strachey, J., 'Some Unconscious Factors in Reading', in *International Journal of Psycho-Analysis*, vol. 11, 1930, pp. 328–30.

86. Ibid., pp. 328–30.

87. Manguel (1996), op. cit., p. 71.

88. The Bible, Proverbs, 5:3.

89. Bettelheim, B. and Zelan, K., *On Learning to Read*, London: Penguin, 1981.

90. Bettelheim, B., *The Uses of Enchantment*, London: Penguin, 1976.

91. Winnicott, D., *Playing and Reality*, London: Penguin, 1971, p. 45.

92. Ibid., p. 113.

93. Ibid., pp. 45, 55, 161.

94. Ibid., p. 60.

95. Ibid., p. 64.

96. Bollas, C., *The Shadow of the Object*, London: Free Association Books, 1987, pp. 34–5.

96. Levi, T., *A Cat Called Adolf*, London: Valentine Mitchell, 1995, p. 11 (first sentence mine).

98. *The Times*, London: 29 January 2001.

99. Olivier, C., *Jocasta's Children*, London: Routledge, 1989, pp. 70, 142, 6–7.

100. Ibid., p. 43.

101. Anon., British pacifist slogan, 1940.

102. Olivier (1989), op. cit., p. 2.

103. Ibid., p. 39.

104. Ibid., p. 103.

105. Ibid., p. 47.

106. Ibid., p. 46.

107. Ibid., pp. 48, 80.

108. Savona, J.L., *Jean Genet*, London: Macmillan, 1983, p. 108.

109. Olivier (1989), op. cit., p. 75.

110. Ibid., p. 75.

111. Ibid., p. 126.

112. Riviere (1929), op. cit., p. 303.

113. *The Guardian*, London: 17 March 2001.

114. Olivier (1989), op. cit., p. 125.

115. Pacteau, F., *The Symptom of Beauty*, London: Reaktion Books, 1994, p. 14.

116. Ibid., p. 16.

117. Ibid., p. 31.

118. Marlowe, C., *Dr Faustus* (1604), V.i; The Bible: Kings, 11:3; The Song of Solomon, 6:13.

119. Pacteau (1994), op. cit., p. 156.

120. Ibid., p. 88.

121. Freud, S., 'Mourning and Melancholia' (1917) PFL 11, p. 258; SE 14, p. 249.

122. Pacteau (1994), op. cit., p. 91.

123. Milner, M., *On Not Being Able to Paint*, London: Heinemann, 1950.

124. Winnicott, D., 'Some Thoughts on the Word Democracy' (1950), in *The Family and Individual Development*, London: Tavistock, 1964.

125. Clendinnen, I., *Reading the Holocaust*, Cambridge: Cambridge University Press, 1999.

126. Borowski, T., *This Way for the Gas, Ladies and Gentlemen*, London: Penguin, 1976.

127. Lanzmann, C., 'The Obscenity of Understanding', in Caruth, C. (ed.), *Trauma: Explorations in Memory*, London: Johns Hopkins University Press, 1995, p. 204.

128. Geoghegan, V., *Reason and Eros: The Social Theory of Herbert Marcuse*, London: Pluto, 1981, pp. 56, 76–8.

129. Lanzmann, in Caruth (1995), op. cit., p. 204.

130. Benjamin, W., *Illuminations*, London: Fontana, 1973, p. 249.

131. Black, E., *IBM and the Holocaust*, London: Little, Brown, 2001.

132. Shorter, E., *A History of Women's Bodies*, London: Allen Lane, 1983.

133. 'Work liberates'; inscribed over the gates of Dachau concentration camp in 1933, and subsequently at Auschwitz and Sachsenhausen camps.

134. Theweleit, K., *Male Fantasies*, Oxford: Polity/Blackwell, 1987, p. 53.

135. Levi, P., *If This Is A Man* (1947), London: Abacus, 1987, p. 17.

136. Salinger, J.D., *The Catcher in the Rye* (1951), London: Penguin, 1984; Levi, P., *The Drowned and the Saved*, London: Abacus, 1988.

Acknowledgements

Ivan Ward's supererogatory care. Duncan Heath and Jeremy Cox for reality checks. The benign guidance of Michael Briant, Lucy King, Mark Phippen, Carole Robinson, and Glenys Scott. The steadying friend's bias of Jim Douglas, Dan Jones, Matthew Jones, Dieter Peetz, Corinna Russell, Wendy Thurley, and Janice Western. Gurnam Iqbal Nanner – the altered ego.

Dedication

For my sisters, Susan Kaur and the late Bakshi Kaur, and my unmet kinsmen, the late Peyla Munda Nanner and Jeremiah Ravinder Wallace.